W9-DES-303

MAKING A BETTER WORLD

Alternative Energy Sources

By Gary Chandler and Kevin Graham

30036001220035

THE FARMINGTON COMMUNITY LIBRARY
FARMINGTON HILLS BRANCH
32737 West Twelve Mile Road
Farmington Hills, MI 48334-3302

Twenty-First Century Books

A Division of Henry Holt and Company
New York

Twenty-First Century Books
A division of Henry Holt and Company, Inc.
115 West 18th Street
New York, New York 10011

Henry Holt® and colophon are registered trademarks of
Henry Holt and Company, Inc.
Publishers since 1866

©1996 by Blackbirch Graphics, Inc.
First Edition
5 4 3 2 1
All rights reserved.
No part of this book may be reproduced in any form without permission
in writing from the publisher, except by a reviewer.

Published in Canada by Fitzhenry & Whiteside Ltd.
195 Allstate Parkway, Markham, Ontario L3R 4T8

Printed in the United States of America on acid free paper.

Created and produced in association with Blackbirch Graphics, Inc.
Series Editor: Tanya Lee Stone

Library of Congress Cataloging-in-Publication Data

Chandler, Gary.
   Alternative energy sources / by Gary Chandler and Kevin Graham.
      p.   cm. — (Making a better world)
   Includes index.
   Summary: Explores varieties of alternative energy resources that are
not destructive to the environment.
   ISBN 0-8050-4621-6
   1. Renewable energy sources—Juvenile literature. [1. Renewable energy
sources.] I. Graham, Kevin. II. Title. III. Series: Making a better world
(New York, N.Y.)
TJ808.2.C37   1996
333.79'4—dc20   96-23065
                                                            CIP
                                                             AC

Table of Contents

Welcome to Making a Better World

Alternative energy refers to power derived from renewable sources such as the Sun and wind—as opposed to the non-renewable energy sources that modern society predominantly uses, such as coal and oil. The Earth has a finite supply of non-renewable resources.

Non-renewable energy sources cause various types of pollution. In contrast, most alternative energy sources are pollution-free. Therefore, alternative sources of energy provide a way to help meet the world population's growing power requirements without damaging the environment.

Although the world may never be able to fulfill all of its energy needs through renewable energy sources, it is a goal worth trying to achieve. And people are working toward that goal. Many advances in the fields of solar- and wind-generated power have been made in recent years, and research efforts continue to press forward on numerous other alternative-energy fronts. For example, although natural gas is a non-renewable resource, it is much cleaner than coal and oil and does not pollute the environment.

Many of the ideas behind today's research are based on ideas first investigated long ago. More than 5,000 years ago, boats fitted with sails were powered by the wind on the Nile River in Egypt. And windmills have been used for hundreds of years as a source of power.

Solar power also has a long history. In 212 B.C., the Greek scientist Archimedes allegedly destroyed a Roman fleet by using a system of mirrors to focus the Sun's rays on enemy ships and set them on fire. More than a thousand years later, the Anasazi Indians of the American Southwest built their cliff dwellings facing southward, relying on the Sun to warm them during the cold winter months. (In the Northern Hemisphere, the orbit of the Earth around the Sun results in considerably more sunlight falling on the southern side of an object.)

All of the books in *Making a Better World* report on people—kids, parents, schools, neighborhoods, and companies—who have decided to get involved in a cause they believe in. Through their dedication, commitment, and dreams, they helped to make ours a better world. Each one of the stories in this book will take you through the steps of what it took for some ordinary people to achieve something extraordinary. Of course, in the space of one book, we can share only a fraction of the wonderful stories that exist. After a long and complicated selection process, we have chosen what we believe are the most exciting subjects to tell you about.

We hope this book will encourage you to learn more about alternative energy sources. Better yet, we hope all the books in this series inspire you to get involved. There are plenty of ways that each individual—including you—can make a better world. You will find some opportunities throughout this book—and there are many others out there waiting for you to discover. If you would like to write to us for more information, the address is Earth News, P.O. Box 101413, Denver, CO, 80250.

Sincerely,

Gary Chandler
and
Kevin Graham

Solar Power

Solar energy is one of the most promising forms of renewable and pollution-free energy. Although the Sun is more than 93 million miles from Earth, it provides a free and plentiful source of clean fuel for renewable energy production. Different devices and technologies have been developed to capture this constant and valuable resource.

Solar-generated power benefits the environment by eliminating the tons of air pollutants produced by electricity that is generated from fossil fuels (mainly coal and oil). For thousands of years, people have used various forms of solar energy.

Sun Powers KTAO's Radio Waves

By using sunshine to transmit its signal, a radio station in New Mexico has increased its potential listening audience tenfold. Thanks to this solar boost, KTAO-FM, located in the small community of Taos, can now reach an audience in New Mexico's capital city of Sante Fe, more than 50 miles away. And in so doing, the station has become the nation's only radio station transmitting solely on solar power.

The ability of the Sun to produce electricity is called the photovoltaic (PV) effect. The system at KTAO-FM uses 140 photovoltaic panels to collect the Sun's energy. One component of PV panels is silicon, an element. When sunlight strikes silicon atoms, its energy knocks electrons loose. The movement of these electrons produces electricity. Many small devices, such as pocket calculators, now rely on PV technology for their energy needs.

The power from the photovoltaic panels for KTAO-FM is stored in a bank of batteries that weighs nearly 45,000 pounds. The batteries are able to hold more than five days' worth of power to transmit the station's signal. (A six-day stretch of sunless weather is unheard of in Taos.) Solar power was not only a wise environmental choice for the station, but a cost-effective alternative.

"I didn't consider alternative energy until I had to," says Brad Hockmeyer, KTAO's owner and general manager. "Conventional power ended up being too expensive, so this became the best way we could get it done."

These huge photovoltaic panels collect the energy that powers the radio station.

The solar system was built on top of 10,800-foot Picuris Peak overlooking Taos, a town in the mountains of northern New Mexico. By transmitting KTAO's signal from such a high elevation, the radio station's potential listening audience grew from 15,000 people to 150,000.

Getting electricity to the top of the mountain via power lines would have cost the radio station at least $300,000. The solar system, though, cost just $60,000.

What is more, the system will save the station about $4,000 a year in traditional electricity costs. So, conceivably, the $60,000 system will pay for itself over 15 years.

"I'd love to get people thinking solar," Hockmeyer says. "The benefit that comes from just thinking of an alternative method—even if they can't do it—is better than not even considering it."

Since hooking up the system, Hockmeyer has been contacted by a number of other radio station owners trying to determine if solar power might be a good option for them. "If this project gets them looking into the possibilities, maybe they'll say, 'Well, I can't do it for my radio station, but I can do it for the hot water heater at my house, or maybe I can use solar energy to power *part* of my radio station.'"

KTAO-FM's Sun logo was created to advertise that the station is run solely on solar power.

For More Information
Write to KTAO, P.O. Box 1844, Taos, NM 87571, or call (505) 758-5826.

Storing Solar Energy

As you have seen, solar-generated power benefits the environment by eliminating the tons of air pollutants that are produced by fossil fuel-generated electricity. Plus, the sunshine used to produce electricity is free. But solar power is not widely used. An important piece of the puzzle to making solar power more reliable and more widely used is storing the energy. That piece is now in place.

The Electric Power Research Institute (EPRI) is working with an electric utility company in southern California and the U.S. Department of Energy on the "Solar Two" project, which is now successfully storing heat energy from the Sun to produce electricity. The $48 million project, which began operating in the summer of 1996 in the California desert, will use thousands of computer-driven mirrors to track the Sun and focus beams of sunlight onto a tower-mounted central receiver. This receiver will absorb the solar energy as heat.

Molten (melted) salt will then be pumped to the top of the receiver tower using pumps powered by electricity, where the salt will be heated by the collected energy. Later, the superheated salt will be used to turn water into steam, which in turn will spin a turbine generator to produce electricity.

During the 1980s, an earlier project, appropriately named Solar One, pumped water to the top of a receiving tower, where it was turned into steam. However, in that system, the steam had to be used immediately to produce electricity, and any cloud cover would slow the system down considerably. To solve this problem, Solar Two turned to hot salt.

Molten salt can easily be stored and will stay hot much longer than steam—which begins to condense back into water minutes later. This improved system is much more efficient. The super-heated salt can turn water to steam many times over and create a steadier production of electricity. For instance, clouds have less of an impact on the system because the super-heated salt will stay hot long enough to keep turning water to steam during periods of cloud cover.

Solar Two demonstrates that clean solar energy is a reliable and economical way to produce large quantities of power. "Any time you can generate electricity from the Sun, you're not generating it from fossil fuel, which means no pollution emissions," notes Ed DeMeo, manager of EPRI's solar program.

The top of the central receiver tower is shown in the reflection of one of the many computer-driven mirrors that focus sunlight onto the receiver.

For More Information
Write to the Electric Power Research Institute, 3412 Hillview Avenue, Palo Alto, CA 94303, or call (415) 855-2159.

Solar Power Helps Utilities Meet Peak Demand

Another California-based electric and gas utility has taken a different approach to solar power. Pacific Gas & Electric Company (PG&E) decided to use the Sun to help solve some of its problems in meeting the high demand for electricity in the summertime. In a joint project with the U.S. Department of Energy, PG&E built a huge photovoltaic system on 5 acres of land near the city of Fresno.

"At full power, the system produces 500 kilowatts of electricity," says Brian Farmer, PG&E's project manager. "And the time frame works well for us because the system is generating power when our demand is peaking in the afternoon."

One hundred and fifty-three solar arrays (groupings) have been set up at the site. Each array has 80 smaller photovoltaic panels. These arrays automatically rotate with the Sun's path, converting sunlight to electricity in the process. The project marks the first time that a photovoltaic system has been used to provide operating and economic benefits to the main electric grid and to generate energy for the utility's customers.

The project's main goal is to determine if PG&E can save money by not adding expensive transformers (devices that convert the high voltage on power lines to voltage customers can use), electric lines, and other electrical equipment to meet peak loads—relying instead on solar power. (Although the source of the power is free, tapping the resource of the Sun is not.) "If utilities can avoid system upgrades, a lot of costs can be

avoided," Farmer says. "This effort will help us find out if that is possible. Even if solar power's operating costs are high now, it's the way of the future because costs should eventually come down."

The Fresno project is part of a larger effort called Photovoltaics for Utility Scale Applications (PVUSA), a cooperative research and development program. Utility companies, the U.S. Department of Energy, and the Electric Power Research Institute are working, through PVUSA, to expand the use of solar power. To date, PVUSA has helped with 19 photovoltaic projects in 6 states.

While these projects are intended mainly for research and demonstration purposes, they are already supplying usable power to America's power grid—although still in small amounts. So

Photovoltaic panels are installed at PVUSA in California.

The PVUSA project tests and maintains a large bank of panels to continue to research solar power.

far, the projects have supplied enough power to satisfy the electricity needs of about 1,000 homes.

PVUSA's main goal is to determine the potential of photo-voltaics in large-scale applications. Because photovoltaic cells (the small units in PV panels that convert sunlight to energy) with 25-year lifetimes are now manufactured—and costs have dropped to a half of what they were ten years ago—PVUSA-backed efforts may soon prove to be cost-effective. Since the technology is silent, emissions-free, and requires no fuel or cooling water, it has almost no impact on the environment.

For More Information

Write to PG&E and PVUSA, 2303 Camino Ramon, Suite 200, San Ramon, CA 94583, or call (510) 866-5259 or (916) 753-0725.

Solar-Sphere Technology
a New Approach

On a smaller scale, a new "solar sphere" approach to photo-voltaic cells has the potential to produce low-cost, clean energy for individual homes.

Ontario Hydro Technologies (OHT) in Toronto, Canada, is developing what it calls Spheral Solar™ technology—a skinlike solar panel. This breakthrough in technology was the result of a $10 million, six-year effort between the electric utility Southern California Edison Company, and Texas Instruments (TI), the Dallas, Texas-based manufacturer of computer equipment and consumer electronics products.

OHT recently bought the solar sphere technology from TI and is continuing to develop it. The material could literally become the skin of many buildings, being integrated into surfaces, much like the roof of a home, rather than being an attachment, as is typically seen today.

OHT believes that, by combining inexpensive and abundant materials with a low-cost manufacturing process, the new technology will be able to produce affordable solar systems for new homes and businesses.

The target cost for a system using these new solar cells is under $3,000, as opposed to the $8,000 to $12,000 with the current technology. This is mainly because Spheral Solar™ uses inexpensive silicon that costs about $1 a pound instead of the $35-a-pound silicon used in other processes.

The technology features a patented process using this low-cost material to create individual, 4-inch-square solar sphere

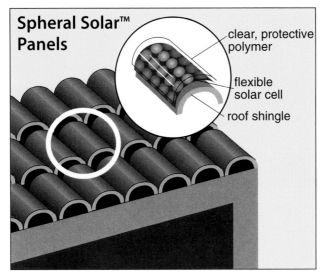

Spheral Solar™ Panels

clear, protective polymer

flexible solar cell

roof shingle

panels. Each panel is composed of 17,000 tiny silicon balls, or spheres, embedded on a thin aluminum foil that makes the finished product flexible, lightweight, and durable. This flexibility allows the cells to be molded into a variety of shapes not previously possible with large conventional solar panels. They don't require the extra protection of glass either, saving more than 65 percent of the weight incurred on conventional photovoltaic modules.

The aluminum serves as both the panel's structure and as conductor for the electricity produced by the spheres. And because each of the 17,000 spheres operates independently, the impact of an individual cell failing is negligible when compared to today's cells.

OHT, which is a subsidiary of Ontario Hydro, North America's largest electrical utility company, is looking at the potential that this technology has for providing an independent electricity generation option. Beyond that, however, are numerous commercial uses and applications.

The modules have been tested outdoors for several years now, with no measurable problems. Once commercial manufacturing begins, the new solar cells could be installed on new homes and buildings. Systems for existing structures would be developed later as manufacturing costs drop.

For More Information

Write to Ontario Hydro Technologies Communications and Public Affairs, 800 Kipling Avenue, Toronto, Ontario, Canada M8Z-554, or call (416) 207-6550.

Cloud Gel Creates a Solar Shutter

Yet another type of solar technology has been created that responds to heat and light and regulates the amount of sunlight that enters a building. This "solar shutter" either uses the Sun for heating and lighting or reflects it for cooling. Its development could revolutionize the housing industry and drastically cut energy consumption.

Suntek Inc., a company based in Albuquerque, New Mexico, has created a substance it calls Cloud Gel. The gluelike mixture is placed between two layers of clear glass or plastic film, which are then used in windows, skylights, greenhouses, and sunrooms.

Cloud Gel stays perfectly clear when a building is cold or when light levels are low, thus allowing in as much sunlight as possible. However, it turns into a reflective white to block the sunlight when a building is too warm or bright inside. By varying the ingredients, the gel can be produced so that it is set to change at any temperature between 68°F to 104°F.

"This change from clear to opaque can occur with only a two-degree rise in temperature," says Suntek president Roy Chahroudi. "With this concept, we cut out many of the negatives of solar. It uses the very skin of a building—supplying both heat and light or rejecting excess heat and light—in a very simple process."

A passive solar system is one that does not use any mechanical means to generate heat. Windows placed on the south side of a house and a greenhouse that is attached to a building are

This model shows how Cloud Gel goes from clear (left) to opaque (right) to block the Sun when a room becomes too warm or bright.

two types of passive solar systems. Suntek has incorporated the use of Cloud Gel into a new product that it calls the Weather Panel—a prefabricated (factory-made) building component. With a roof made of Weather Panels, a passive solar house is simple to design and build. The Weather Panel also uses several other solar technologies invented by Suntek to save energy.

Suntek initially plans to sell the technology that makes the Weather Panels possible to various building-materials manufacturers, who will manufacture and sell them. Several companies are now testing the panels.

"We're a company of only ten people, but we've developed a product that could save one sixth of the world's energy consumption," Chahroudi says. "We're in this to enable world energy consumption to be reduced."

Salt-Laden Timbers Create Plenty of Free Heat

Salt supplies the impetus for another solar-heating idea that spares the environment and has won a U.S. Department of Energy award for innovation. One night, Michael Sykes sat down on a pile of driftwood at a North Carolina beach. He was amazed at the heat the wood still retained from the Sun well after dark.

Sykes realized that the salt in the wood was helping hold in the heat, as it does in other applications. And being a builder of log homes, he also thought that he might have struck on an idea for a new way to heat them.

He soon formed a company called Enertia Building Systems in Wake Forest, North Carolina. The company builds homes using salt-impregnated timbers and a unique design that cuts energy costs for heating by 90 percent over those of conventional homes.

"When I initially built log homes, I noticed that they retained heat for three or four days," Sykes explains. "That led to the idea of combining salt-treated wood and either solar heat or a wood stove to create a house with few or no heating requirements."

A prototype (model) Enertia home in New Hampshire was compared to a similar home next door. While the Enertia home had no heating costs during the winter, the house next door needed $3,000 worth of heating oil. The physical property that allows mass—in this case, wood—to retain heat is called thermal inertia. For his company name, Sykes decided

19

to change the first letter in "inertia" to "e" to denote the environment and energy.

An Enertia home relies on a unique air loop for heating, created by a double-shell design. Air is circulated through the outer shell of the house to distribute heat evenly. On the south side of an Enertia home, an 8-foot-wide room is built with glass on the outer wall and salt-treated timbers on the inner wall. Air is heated in this space and rises, recharging the home's thermal battery.

On the north side, the space between two log walls is only 8 inches, and as the air cools, it is pulled down and eventually circulated back to the south side. A simple ceiling fan assists this natural air loop. Solar heat is stored in the salt-laden timbers and slowly released over time, keeping the loop in motion.

An Enertia house is built with salt-treated wood that retains heat from the Sun.

The Enertia houses are made from 20-year-old pines bought from nearby tree plantations, so no old-growth forest is destroyed. These timbers also replace the need for drywall, vinyl siding, and insulation used on the outer walls of more conventional homes.

So far, more than 30 Enertia houses have been built in more than a dozen states, and the company is building a factory to mass-produce the structures. The houses are precut, with timbers being numbered, grooved, and packaged in the order that they will be needed. Owners put in an insulated basement foundation and install a roof of their choice.

"Our effort helps the environment because we drastically cut the use of petroleum-based housing materials in our construction," Sykes says. "And we're replacing houses that use plenty of energy for heating and cooling—pulling them off the market one by one."

This finished Enertia house is complete with a solar-powered lawnmower in the front yard!

For More Information

Write to Enertia Building Systems, 13312 Garffe Sherron Road, Wake Forest, NC 27587, or call (919) 556-0177, or visit them on the Internet at http://enertia.com

Using Solar Energy for Light

Greg Miller's 85-year-old uncle wanted some natural light in his kitchen. However, he didn't want the expense of installing a typical skylight, so he started considering alternatives.

Miller joined his uncle in this search, and the men soon struck on an idea they call the SunPipe. It's not really a new idea. The ancient Egyptians used gold- and silver-lined shafts to bring light down into their stone structures. The SunPipe is an offshoot of this design.

"The biggest job and expense of a skylight is building the shaft or well to bring light from the rooftop down to the ceiling of a room inside a house," says Miller, president and founder of the SunPipe Company. "But the SunPipe is its own inexpensive, super-reflective shaft. A silver film lamination in the pipe creates a mirrored surface that brings a lot of light into a building. The film was developed for use in the solar-energy field."

Unlike a skylight, which allows a beam of light into a room, the SunPipe reflects sunlight down to a dome, mounted in the ceiling, and light is scattered throughout a room like an electric light fixture. In the middle of the summer at Chicago, Illinois' latitude, a SunPipe will produce the equivalent light of fifteen 100-watt lightbulbs. In the winter, the light production drops off, but the SunPipe will still produce 400 to 500 watts of light—plenty for a kitchen or living room.

SunPipes sell in 13-inch and 21-inch diameter versions. Although the 21-inch model allows in so much light that it is too bright for most houses, it is perfect for use in larger buildings.

Using the Sun to provide light can produce huge benefits for the environment. About 25 percent of all energy produced in the United States now goes toward lighting.

"Our true environmental impact lies in the commercial and industrial market," Miller explains. "With several 21-inch SunPipes and adequate daylight, businesses can keep their lights off. In many parts of the United States, companies could save huge amounts of electric lighting energy. And no supplemental air conditioning is needed because any heat produced is ventilated out the top of the pipe."

A SunPipe kit includes everything needed to install the unit except the pipe, tools, and caulk for the roof. Pipe length usually varies depending on the roof. Installation typically takes between two and four hours.

The company has also created a SunScoop. This device attaches to the top of a SunPipe and directs additional sunlight into the reflective shaft. By facing south, the SunScoop can increase light output by 10 percent in the summer and up to 300 percent during the winter.

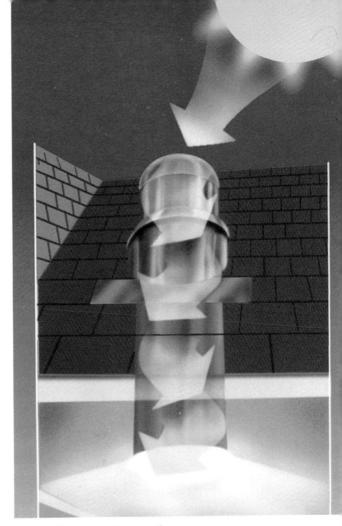

SunPipes work by funneling light down through a shaft built into a roof and scattering that light.

For More Information

Write to the SunPipe Company, P.O. Box 2223, Northbrook, IL 60065, or call (800) 844-4786.

Harnessing the Power of the Wind

*I*t drives golfers mad, puts millions of kites in the air, and has powered sailboats for centuries. It is the wind—a renewable source of power that is poised to produce more and more electric energy in the coming years.

As the cost of producing wind-powered electricity continues to drop due to technological advances that capture wind power more efficiently, interest in this renewable-energy source is whipping up. The true challenge for wind power is to be economically competitive with oil, coal, and natural gas in producing electricity.

Thanks to new technology, wind power is now as cost-efficient as conventional sources of energy. This fact, along with steadily improving technology, has set the stage for a potential major commercial thrust in the use of wind power.

Technology Center Pushes
Wind Energy Ahead

Under average wind conditions, a 100-kilowatt wind turbine (a machine that changes the motion of the wind into rotary motion) produces enough electricity to meet the residential power needs of about 50 people. Across the entire United States, more than 15,000 wind turbines produce more than 2 million kilowatts of electricity each year, enough power for 1 million people. But most of these turbines are already outdated and are not using some of the new technology that has dramatically boosted the power produced by more advanced turbines. For example, new blade designs developed at the National Renewable Energy Laboratory (NREL) have increased the energy output of some new turbines by up to 25 percent. And technology has reduced the cost of wind energy from more than 50 cents per kilowatt hour to about 5 cents per kilowatt hour.

Run by the NREL, the refurbished National Wind Technology Center reopened its doors in 1994 to continue bolstering wind-turbine research and development. It is situated at the foot of the Rocky Mountains south of Boulder, Colorado.

"The center is attracting scientists and manufacturers who share the dream of widespread, economical wind power," says Robert Thresher, director of the center. "Ultimately, we hope that companies seeking to develop the vast wind resources of the Great Plains will find this area a logical place to locate a corporate facility or manufacturing plant."

*An aerial view
of the National
Wind Technology
Center near
Boulder*

"Wind is expected to become one of the least expensive forms of new electric generation in the next century," says Thresher. "At good sites, wind power will be widely competitive by the year 2000. We're pretty close, but the industry needs continued support in research and development efforts because most wind companies are small businesses that are just starting out."

Utility companies and wind developers across the country have plans to produce more than 4,200 megawatts of new wind generation by the year 2006, in 15 U.S. states (using a much smaller number of turbines to do so). In blustery North Dakota alone, estimates suggest that wind sites could produce more than 30 percent of the total electricity that was consumed by the United States in 1990.

The National Wind Technology Center will accommodate up to 16 wind turbines and allow numerous companies to work on their various wind products. Four turbines have already been constructed at the center, and when it is fully utilized by the end of the century, up to 5 megawatts of power could be generated.

A wind-technology facility was built at the Colorado site in 1981, but when the Reagan administration slashed the renewable-energy budget in the early 1980s, activity at the center was drastically reduced. However, the Bush and Clinton administrations provided for increased renewable-energy budgets and the site was refurbished and fully reoccupied in 1994. Today, the center encompasses nearly 300 acres of land at Rocky Flats, a large, elevated plain south of Boulder.

NREL liked the site because it is in an area that experiences two distinct wind patterns. During the fall and winter, powerful winds sweep over the Continental Divide and down the mountains, reaching speeds of more than 120 miles per hour and producing severe conditions in which to test the durability of wind turbines. In the spring, consistent and smoother winds blow in from the east and northeast, providing operating conditions similar to those of the plains in the Midwest, where the winds sweep across the land.

Scientists and engineers can use computer models at the center to simulate operating wind turbines and individual components. The laboratory space at the facility is large enough to allow for the disassembly of large turbines so that their individual components can be analyzed and modified.

"The site is designed not only to be a center for research, but a technology magnet for a new industry as well," Thresher explains. It's a place where NREL scientists are working side by side with wind-turbine developers to create the advanced systems of the future. It is also where wind-plant operators and utility companies can come for technical assistance. Adds

NREL workers adjust these wind turbine blades during a test.

Thresher, "Our reason for being here is to perform research on wind technology and assist the industry in making wind power a cost-effective option."

For More Information

Write to the National Wind Technology Center, c/o National Renewable Energy Laboratory, 1617 Cole Boulevard, Golden, CO 80401, or call (303) 384-6950.

Addressing Concerns About Bird Deaths

The source of wind power is free, and it produces no air or water pollution. However, one drawback of wind turbines is that they sometimes kill birds that fly into the spinning blades.

A two-year study completed in 1992 considered the impact of wind turbines on birds at California's Altamont Pass, the site of the world's single largest wind farm (a "farm" that produces wind power). There, thousands of turbines occupy 20,000 acres of land located 50 miles east of San Francisco. Of the 183 dead birds found over the course of the study, 111 were raptors, or birds of prey. They included red-tailed hawks, American kestrels, and golden eagles.

Just over half of their deaths were attributed to collisions with turbines, and the study also suggested that golden eagles could be dying at an alarming rate. Besides being less abundant than the other raptor species in the area, golden eagle breeding rates are also slower. Thus, turbine deaths could be especially troublesome to this prized species.

Bird deaths are hard to track and record though, so no one is quite sure of the impact that wind farms are having on raptor populations. The wind industry states that, according to its research, about one raptor a year is killed for every 100 turbines in use.

Statistics like these put the U.S. Fish and Wildlife Service in a tough position. Mike Jennings, a biologist working for the service in Wyoming, where a new wind farm is planned for the state's windy southern plains, says, "It's difficult because we

A red-tailed hawk is released in order to track its flight around turbines.

support wind power but are also responsible for enforcing laws set up to protect various bird species. We support the idea but must suggest modifications that slow its progress. It can be a dilemma."

To shed more light on this dilemma, another study is under way to look at the overall effects on the golden eagle population around Altamont Pass rather than just the number of deaths. The National Wind Technology Center and the Audubon Society are involved in the study, which is being conducted by the University of California at Santa Cruz.

This study will determine estimates of the total eagle population living in the area as well as eagles that travel through the region sporadically. It then will estimate the yearly mortality rates caused by turbines and the resulting impact of those deaths on the overall population.

More than 100 golden eagles of all ages have been tagged with radio transmitters and are being monitored. When one of the transmitters does not move for more than four hours, a mortality sensor is activated, warning of a possible death.

"The only way to really get at what's happening to the birds is to look at their overall population—is it growing or getting smaller? The population is the main thing," says Robert Thresher, director of the center. "Wind farms may end up occupying land that otherwise would be occupied by building developments that could end up being more harmful to the species."

Patterns designed to increase the visibility of wind turbine blades were tested successfully in California.

Nonetheless, steps are already being taken by the wind-power industry to minimize the impact that wind farms have on local bird populations, particularly various species of raptors. Kenetech Windpower, for example, the largest developer of wind energy systems in the world, has spent more than $2 million on research and specific improvements to make its wind farms safer for birds of prey. The company plans to use long, straight, tubular towers for its turbines instead of the lattice-type towers installed in the past. The lattice structures attract the birds because they provide numerous perching spots. In addition, perch guards are now being placed on these older structures.

Kenetech has also avoided putting ladders and catwalks on the new tubular towers, as they also provide perching spots. Instead, the company will conduct maintenance on the turbines from bucket trucks—vehicles with "cherry pickers" similar to those used by telephone and other utility companies. Other innovative techniques include painting the turbine blades in patterns or different colors to make them more visible to raptors and other birds.

"Patterns will be installed on the blades used at the Wyoming site," Jennings says. "When spinning, we hope the blades will look like a solid visual obstruction to the birds. We know we'll never completely eliminate bird mortality, but we're working at minimizing wind power's impact. The Wyoming project will be a model for many of these new ideas. We hope they cut mortalities and keep them so low that it's not a problem. We're working with industry to get the best technology in place with each new facility."

For More Information

Write to the U.S. Fish and Wildlife Service, 4000 Morrie Avenue, Cheyenne, WY 82001.

Turbines and Electricity

Of the many ways that electricity can be created, a number of methods rely on the same end process: the use of a turbine generator. The difference lies in how the turbine is spun to create the electricity.

When coal is used as a fuel, for instance, the first step involves burning the coal to heat water and turn it into steam. This steam then turns blades—similar to those on a windmill—that are attached to a turbine shaft.

Connected to the end of the turbine shaft is a piece of machinery that is made of iron called a rotor. Around the outside of the rotor is another piece of iron machinery called a stator. Coils of copper wire make up a large part of the stator.

When the rotor spins inside the stator, electricity is created. The rotor and stator together are called the generator.

For the Solar Two project (mentioned in Chapter One), a turbine generator is used to create electricity—just like in a coal-fired power plant. But in the Solar Two effort, the Sun, rather than coal, is used to heat water and make steam. In this way, the pollution that would have been created by burning coal does not exist.

Similarly, wind turbines use a form of the standard turbine generator to create electricity. In this case, however, the turbine shaft is spun by wind power instead of steam power. And again, the wind—just like the Sun and volcanic heat—is capable of producing electricity without creating pollution.

Wind Company Expands
Its Horizons

Along with its work to control bird mortality, Kenetech Windpower's recent innovations in technology are allowing the company to work on numerous projects with various utility companies in the United States and Canada. The Department of Energy (DOE) estimates that wind energy could eventually supply nearly 20 percent of America's electricity needs. Although much of the country's wind power currently is produced in California, the wind-power arena is primed to expand. Many other areas of the country offer equal or better wind sites than those in California.

"We are certainly keeping our eyes open to all parts of the country in trying to expand wind-driven power plants," says Alexander Ellis, Kenetech's vice-president of marketing. "We've identified 13 states that have even better wind than California."

Kenetech has designed a variable-speed turbine that overcomes problems encountered by earlier, constant-speed versions. Frequent and severe changes in wind speeds create problems for constant-speed turbines. Maintenance costs are also high. However, a variable-speed turbine allows the rotor and generator to accelerate easily in higher winds to avoid damage while assuring a consistent electric load for utility companies.

Kenetech also has created a concept called a Windplant— a large group of interconnected wind turbines that operate as a single power plant. This computer-based system permits automatic and independent operation of each turbine while controlling hundreds—or even thousands—of wind turbines as a single unit. Under this concept, turbines can be added in small amounts as energy demand grows. In addition, individual turbines can be serviced at scheduled intervals, eliminating the need to shut down the entire Windplant.

A stand-alone wind-power system can provide enough energy to significantly raise the standard of living for many of the developing world's poorest rural people. One turbine with battery storage capability can handle services such as refrigeration, water pumping, water treatment, grain grinding, communications, and power for a school or community center.

"We have a small but active program for developing world applications aimed at using small wind turbines," says National Wind Technology Center director Robert Thresher. "We also are studying another system—a powerhouse that uses renewable energy from the wind, along with batteries and a diesel

The Kenetech Windplant has underground cables (shown in the cut-out in the earth) that connect all the turbines to a central computer station (inset).

Variable-speed wind turbines allow small wind farms to produce effective power.

generator. This backup generator would run the system when sufficient wind resources are not available."

Called a village power system, the unit can be shipped overseas in a steel shipping container, then can be loaded onto a truck for delivery. As compared to stand-alone diesel generators, these systems cost less in the long run, are better for the environment, and are more reliable. "These people have no power now, and renewables can provide that power," Thresher explains. "We're getting a lot of interest from developing countries. In essence, it involves bettering people's lives."

For More Information

Write to Kenetech Windpower, 500 Sansome Street, San Francisco, CA 94111, or call (415) 398-3825.

Other Forms of Clean Energy

*T*he bulk of research and business efforts to increase the use of alternative energy currently centers on solar and wind power, but other types of renewable energy are also being investigated closely. Ideas such as using the heat stored inside the Earth to create steam and collecting methane gas produced by landfills to heat buildings are two such endeavors. As with the Sun and wind, the purpose is to create energy without producing pollution or using nonrenewable resources such as coal or oil.

Tapping the Earth's Energy

To date, drilling into the Earth for energy has typically involved exploration for, or extraction of, oil and natural gas—both non-renewable resources. But a renewable source of energy from the Earth's crust is now being investigated.

Called hot-dry-rock (HDR) energy, the technology involves tapping the dry heat stored in rock formations deep underground. This energy source is both clean and virtually inexhaustible.

Geothermal energy—naturally occurring underground water sources tapped for their steam—provides the basis for understanding hot-dry-rock technology. But while geothermal energy relies on hot water already present underground, HDR technology pumps cool water down one well about 12,000 feet into the Earth, lets the rock heat the water, and then draws the resulting steam back up to the surface through a second well. The water is pumped into the Earth and returned to the surface using electricity.

Since 1974, HDR technology has been studied at the Los Alamos National Laboratory in Los Alamos, New Mexico. At a site just west of the lab, called Fenton Hill, testing has been conducted at a pilot plant since 1986.

The plant's first test produced 4 megawatts of geothermal heat on a continuous basis for four months. Water was pumped down the first well at 57°F and returned up the second well quite a bit warmer—365°F.

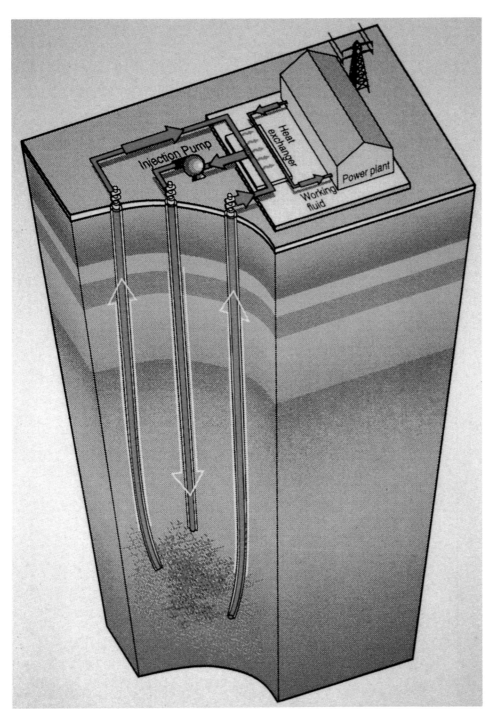

Labels on illustration: Injection Pump, Heat exchanger, Working fluid, Power plant

This illustration shows how an HDR mine works. A high-pressure pump forces water down a well, through hot rock to absorb the thermal energy, and then up one or more additional wells.

This steam was produced from the Fenton Hill HDR heat mine.

"Environmentally, this technology holds a lot of promise, because there are no pollutants involved," says project manager David Duchane. "As we learn to do this, small power plants could be built at sites where the power is needed. I think it's the most promising source of energy we have for the future."

Although water loss was a concern at first, it is now believed that the technology will eventually allow for only a 3 percent water loss, due to a nearly closed-loop energy system that uses very little water.

The next step in HDR technology is to construct a production plant in conjunction with private industry and then market the electricity or heat produced.

"If we can demonstrate that this technology can produce power economically, we'll be on our way," Duchane explains. "There are enough high-grade rock resources in the United States to supply all of the country's electricity needs well into the future."

The first electric-producing HDR plant is expected to go into production just after the turn of the century. And if all goes well, the technology could be widely accepted as an energy alternative by 2010.

"There are no real technical obstacles to overcome like you have with fusion and other technologies," says Duchane. "We've already proven that it can work. Now we need to make it work economically—that's the next step."

For More Information

Write to the Los Alamos National Laboratory, Mail Stop D443, Los Alamos, NM 87545, or call (505) 667-9893.

Capturing Landfill Gas

A closed-down landfill may seem an unusual energy source for supplying heating and cooling to a manufacturing plant. But that's just what is taking place at an American Telephone & Telegraph (AT&T) manufacturing facility in Columbus, Ohio. For the next 30 years or so, AT&T will rely on methane gas from the landfill to heat and cool its massive 50-acre facility, where 6,000 people are employed.

Methane—a naturally occurring by-product of landfills—is a gas that is produced as garbage decomposes. Methane can drift into the atmosphere and is a contributing factor to the global warming problem. Global warming, also known as the greenhouse effect, is the phenomemon of atmospheric heating in which carbon dioxide and other gases act like glass in a greenhouse roof by trapping more and more of the Sun's heat and causing increasing warming on Earth. A warmer world could have devastating effects, scientists believe, such as extreme weather patterns and rising oceans. By tapping methane as an energy source, Network Energy is helping to keep harmful gases from polluting the environment.

A pipeline supervisor fuses (connects with heat) special plastic pipe for a Network Energy pipeline.

A completed Network Energy well

In one year, the huge AT&T facility, which produces cellular products for worldwide distribution, will use the amount of gas needed to heat 2,000 homes for a year.

Network Energy, a company that specializes in methane gas-recovery projects, installed a unique collection and transmission system. The methane gas produced by the 70-acre landfill is collected by a series of wells. Holes are drilled 50 feet deep, then perforated pipe is inserted to collect the gas. Each well has a valve to turn the flow on and off, like a natural gas well.

The gas flows to a station where it is compressed. It is then shipped via a mile-long underground pipeline to the AT&T facility's boilers. A special burner at the boilers allows AT&T to burn methane or a mixture of methane and natural gas.

AT&T saved about $60,000 in fuel costs in the methane system's first year of operation alone. And a brick manufacturing company in the same area uses methane gas from the same landfill to power its kiln.

"We can supply an alternative fuel to customers and save them money on their natural gas bills," says Network Energy's Jeff Blanton. "And on top of that, we're allowing them to take a positive step in controlling landfill-gas pollution and turn a potential problem into a valuable energy source."

Network Energy has developed four similar methane gas-recovery projects. There are approximately 150 such projects operating in the United States.

For More Information

Write to Network Energy, P.O. Box 110226, Pittsburgh, PA 15232, or call (412) 683-3313.

Clean-Coal Technology Provides Environmental Benefits

Coal is an abundant fuel source available to generate electricity. Unfortunately, burning coal causes a number of types of pollution. But under a U.S. government program, new technologies are creating ways to burn coal that are less harmful for the environment.

Appropriately called the Clean Coal Program, the U.S. Department of Energy (DOE) effort is helping utility companies develop technologies aimed at reducing a number of different types of polluting emissions. Some clean-coal technologies have been able to cut certain pollutants by more than 50 percent. The DOE is matching utility company funding with loans to help encourage the companies to create and investigate ways to cut pollution created by coal-burning power plants.

In the Clean Coal Program, the DOE provides funding for up to half of a project's cost. The loans are intended to be repaid from the eventual sale of the various technologies. The federal government's goal is to help the utility industry develop new pollution-control systems and then release the information, enabling other companies to design and use similar systems.

One of the technologies now being tested is dry-sodium injection, a process aimed at reducing sulfur dioxide emissions. A sodium-based powder is blown into the flue gas that escapes after coal has been burned to create steam. Virtually the same as common baking soda, this mineral reacts with sulfur dioxide to form a particulate—a tiny particle, like a speck of dirt—that can be removed from the gas through other pollution-control

43

Fossil Fuels and Pollution

Relying on fossil fuels, or nonrenewable energy sources, to create electricity is the primary way that modern society generates power. However, renewable forms of energy are beginning to grow in popularity.

Fossil fuels used to create power include coal, oil, and natural gas. All are burned in power plants in order to heat water and create steam, which in turn spins a rotor to create electricity through the use of an electric generator.

The problem with fossil fuels is that they cause pollution, even though steps are being taken to reduce their impact. Burning fossil fuels also creates carbon dioxide. This gas has been pegged as a major contributor to the Earth's growing global warming problem. When compared to pollution-free solar, wind, or geothermal power, fossil fuels are not preferable.

measures. This keeps the sulfur dioxide from escaping into the atmosphere, where it contributes to smog and acid rain. (Acid rain is precipitation that contains high levels of acid-forming chemicals.)

Another effort involves the use of low nitrogen-oxide burners. These special burners allow for more control in mixing coal and air while firing a boiler to create steam and eventually produce electricity.

When a Clean Coal test project is completed, a final report is submitted by the participating utility company to the DOE. This report summarizes cost, construction, and pollution-reduction findings. The DOE then makes the information available to all U.S. power plant operators.

Earthships Require No Energy

The beginnings of Michael Reynolds's unique concept for a new type of house sprouted from a television set in the late 1960s. While watching news anchor Walter Cronkite's broadcast one evening, he saw a story about steel cans. At the time, all beverage containers were made of steel—not aluminum—and the reporter explained that these cans were being thrown everywhere and causing a trash problem.

Cronkite followed this news story with a piece on the timber industry and housing. With all the new houses and buildings being constructed across the country, Cronkite predicted that America's forests were headed for trouble.

"Those two stories sparked an idea in me," Reynolds says. "I was just out of the University of Cincinnati's architecture school and had done my thesis on housing. Within days of that broadcast, I was working on a building block made of steel cans."

Reynolds succeeded in building a house of steel cans by relying on a concrete mixture in the building process. He then decided to take a new tack, using old tires filled with dirt instead of cans as the walls of his next house, which he dubbed an "Earthship."

Reynolds eventually developed a new type of home that takes nothing from the Earth to build or operate. His idea is allowing homeowners the chance to construct and own a completely self-sufficient dwelling anywhere they please. He has since founded a company called Solar Survival Architecture in Taos, New Mexico, to promote the concept. (The KTAO radio station in New Mexico houses its battery supply inside an Earthship.)

To complete the outer walls of an Earthship, tire after tire is filled with dirt, which is then rammed by a sledgehammer until tightly packed. Each dirt-filled tire acts like a 400-pound brick encased in rubber and provides excellent insulation. Layer after layer of tires is piled up until a U-shaped frame of a house is created. To give the house a more conventional look, the 3-foot-thick tire walls are covered with stucco or adobe mud.

An Earthship needs little or no energy for heating or cooling because of these thick walls. While it may take several months for one of the homes to reach 70°F, once there, the

This exterior view of an Earthship built by Solar Survival shows the dirt-filled tire walls before they are covered with stucco.

house will maintain that temperature. An Earthship is its own heating and cooling unit, using the principle of thermal mass. During the day, the cool earth walls absorb heat from the rooms. During the night, they release it again. The U-shaped frame helps to promote the circulation of heat.

Each home faces south, where a glass wall conducts heat inside the dwelling. Interior walls for an Earthship use Reynolds's initial idea of steel cans with a concrete mixture covering. "The use of recycled materials as building products is a direct

The thick walls of an Earthship home provide it with a constantly maintained comfortable temperature.

47

benefit to the environment," he observes. "And they make perfect building materials."

Hundreds of Earthships have been built across the United States, as well as in Japan, Bolivia, Australia, and New Zealand. Hundreds more are now under construction. The homes can be so simple to construct that practically anyone can build one. A family of four in Minnesota once built an Earthship in two months for roughly $12,000 using an instruction book published by Solar Survival. The company often assists homeowners in the building process, however, to ensure that they are made correctly and will function properly.

Mechanical systems within the homes also benefit the environment. Earthships do not require being connected to public utilities. Solar energy can be used for power and light in the dwelling, and a rainwater-catchment system can provide water. Also, by using solar or composting toilets, the need to tie into a septic tank or sewage system is avoided. All of these innovations are taught by Solar Survival.

In addition, by incorporating a greenhouse into the structure or simply using floor space on the south side of the house for plants, Earthship owners can grow their own vegetables and flowers. Reynolds suggests using a system to collect gray water—used water from sinks, showers, and washing machines—to nourish the plants.

Solar Survival Architecture offers a number of avenues to help interested people learn more about Earthships. Periodic training seminars are conducted, and several books have been published to provide information about the structures and give how-to advice on their construction. It also gives tours during the summer months.

For More Information

Write to Solar Survival Architecture, P.O. Box 1041, Taos, New Mexico 87571, or call (505) 758-9870.

CHAPTER

FOUR

New Ways to Power Vehicles

*A*s long ago as 1912, alternative fuels powered many American vehicles. Nearly 40 percent of the vehicles in the United States ran on electric batteries back then, and only 22 percent used gasoline. The rest were steam-powered.

A simple device then turned the tide toward more gasoline-powered vehicles: the electric starter. Gasoline-powered cars could now start up at once, unlike steam-powered vehicles, which needed time to heat up to a required pressure. In addition, gasoline-powered vehicles could be refueled much more easily than electric cars.

Most of the cars, trucks, and buses on the roads today operate by burning gasoline. This produces a lot of pollution. Vehicle emissions cause smog and a number of other air-pollution problems. Although laws concerning emissions have helped to drastically reduce the pollution per vehicle, the number of vehicles on the road has doubled since 1970. Fortunately, new technologies are being developed and innovative ideas being investigated that will allow vehicles of all types to pollute less by running on alternative fuels.

Clean Energy for the Road Ahead

Even though natural gas is a non-renewable resource, it does have one major advantage over other fossil fuels—it is clean and does not pollute the environment. Because of this, natural gas is now being used to power cars, trucks, buses and other vehicles. According to the American Gas Association and the NGV (natural gas vehicles) Coalition, Russia has 315,000 vehicles on the road fueled with natural gas, followed by Argentina with 265,000, Italy with 250,000, and New Zealand with 43,200. The United States has 40,000 and Canada has 20,000.

Italy easily claims the oldest NGV program. Natural gas has fueled Italian cars, trucks, and buses since 1935. Limited quantities of petroleum during World War II forced Italy to create a market for natural gas-powered vehicles. The country now boasts about 240 fueling stations.

In addition, a number of countries are planning expanded NGV programs. These include Indonesia (100,000 additional vehicles by the year 2000), Thailand (50,000), and Pakistan (21,000).

Because gasoline vehicles are a significant source of air pollution in the United States, more and more urban areas with air pollution problems are turning to NGVs to help reduce smog. Gasoline-powered cars, vans, trucks, and buses contribute about three fourths of the carbon monoxide pollution found in urban areas. They also produce most of the hydrocarbons and a significant amount of nitrogen oxides. These gases, when combined in the presence of sunlight, form ground-level ozone. According to the Environmental Protection

Agency, approximately 62 million Americans in 1994 lived in counties with air quality that did not meet national standards.

Using natural gas instead of gasoline is one of the best ways to reduce harmful air pollutants because vehicles fueled with natural gas can reduce emissions of the carbon monoxide and reactive hydrocarbons that contribute to smog by 70 to 90 percent. In addition, NGVs emit virtually none of the tailpipe soot usually associated with vehicles powered by gasoline or diesel fuel.

In addition to its environmental benefits, natural gas usually costs less than gasoline and has an octane rating of 120, much higher than gasoline. This makes it healthier for your car, too.

Vehicles can either be factory-built or converted to operate on natural gas. In addition, cars can be made to run exclusively on natural gas, as dual-fuel vehicles that use both natural gas and gasoline simultaneously, or as bi-fueled vehicles that can run on either fuel.

This school bus is refueling with natural gas during a "Clean Across America" event that demonstrated the benefits of NGVs.

The Clean Air Gas Company operates a fleet of natural gas taxis in Washington, D.C.

NGVs are fueled with natural gas at dispensing pumps that resemble gasoline pumps. Most of the 1,100 natural gas fueling stations nationwide are open to the public.

Most NGVs are used in fleets that share a central fueling station. For example, the U.S. Postal Service operates the world's largest civilian fleet of NGVs, with more than 7,000 vehicles on the road. United Parcel Service (UPS) fuels 230 of its delivery trucks with natural gas, and dozens of smog-plagued cities use natural gas to power their transit buses and school buses to reduce air pollution.

In fact, the "school bus of the future" is powered by natural gas. The low-pollution yellow school bus, developed by the U.S. Department of Energy and several private manufacturers, provides a clean ride for students. It also has safety features such as seat belts, wider aisles for handicapped access, and automotive radar devices to detect pedestrians and vehicles. More than 9,000 school buses are currently fueled with natural gas. This natural gas concept could be the model for future school bus manufacturing.

For More Information

Write to the American Gas Association, 1515 Wilson Boulevard, Arlington, VA 22209, or call (703) 841-8660.

New Station Allows Electric Vehicles to Use Solar Power

Electricity provides yet another alternative fuel for vehicles. Preparing for an increase of electric cars on California's roadways, the capital city of Sacramento has unveiled 20 public electric vehicle charging stations, including the first public, solar-powered, electric-charging station in the western United States. The solar electric-vehicle (EV) "filling station" will serve as a prototype for future stations, both in Sacramento and other parts of the country.

"A lot of people are talking about electric cars in the future, but SMUD [Sacramento Municipal Utility District] is working today to prepare for a large number of EVs on Sacramento's roadways," says Mike Wirsch, manager of electric transportation for SMUD. "EVs are the key to our clean-air future. As the company supplying the fuel for these cars, we have to start preparing now. In sunny Sacramento, it makes sense to use the clean energy of the Sun to make electric vehicles a reality. We want to be an example for the nation."

General Motors, Honda, and Toyota have all announced plans to have EVs ready for sale in 1997. By the year 2003, according to regulations adopted by the California Air Resources Board, 10 percent of all new cars offered for sale in California must be non-polluting vehicles—that's almost 200,000 cars per year! Currently, only electric vehicles fit that profile. Therefore, thousands of EVs will likely be on the state's roads in the very near future.

53

The cost of charging an EV will be much less than using gasoline in conventional cars. By installing charging stations at such places as grocery stores, businesses, public garages, and theaters, SMUD is making battery charging convenient and EVs easy to use as well. The solar charging station is one example of a public charging station. This station uses eight photovoltaic panels that convert the Sun's energy directly into electricity while the car is shaded from the Sun, keeping the car cool during hot days. The solar panels produce a total of 12 kilowatts of electricity per hour and are capable of charging up to eight compact sedans using only renewable energy.

Converters change the direct current from the sun into alternating current (AC), a form of electrical current, which in turn is used to charge EV batteries. Recharging an electric car battery takes between two and eight hours, depending upon the car and the type of batteries it uses.

Even on cloudy days, the solar panels of the charging station can collect enough energy to at least partially charge EVs.

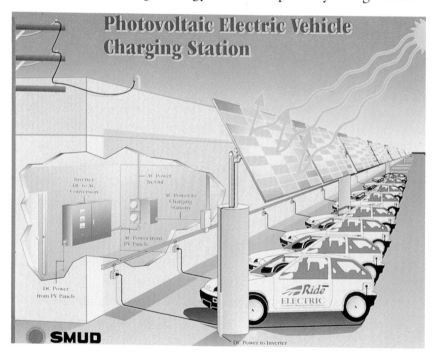

Photovoltaic Electric Vehicle Charging Station

Inverter DC to AC Conversion

AC Power In/Out

AC Power to Charging Stations

AC Power from PV Panels

DC Power from PV Panels

Ride ELECTRIC

SMUD

DC Power to Inverter

When the Sun sets, the EVs can still get a full recharge because the station is hooked up to SMUD's electric system as well. And if the station is not being used to charge batteries, power produced by the solar panels is fed into the district's electric grid.

These electric cars are being charged at the photovoltaic station at SMUD.

"Giving the public better access to electric-vehicle recharging facilities is critical to make the transition to cleaner-fueled vehicles," says Vic Fazio, a U.S. congressional representative from California. "This will help put more electric vehicles on the road, and that means less air pollution and less reliance on imported oil."

For More Information
Write to the Sacramento Municipal Utility District, P.O. Box 15830, MS A-351, Sacramento, CA 95852-1830, or call (916) 732-5486.

Pedestal Power Coming
for Electric Vehicles

There is more news on the electric-vehicle front: A simple-to-use power pedestal that charges electric cars could be one of the initial building blocks for the upcoming electric vehicle industry. As explained earlier, California has passed legislation that sets up a zero-emissions car quota for the state—meaning that electric vehicles are on the way. The states of New York and Massachusetts have passed similar measures.

The Bifronic Power Pedestal Charging Station, developed by Paul Moerman of San Luis Obispo, California, comes completely prewired and can be installed by one person. It weighs only 110 pounds and can restore more than 50 percent power to a discharged EV battery in only three hours. The compact size allows it to be installed at a residential home, for convenient use.

A green light on the 5-foot-tall pedestal tells users when the power is on, and an orange light indicates that the charger is properly connected to the EV. One power pedestal can charge up to four electric vehicles at a time.

Moerman's initial idea for a power pedestal involved the construction industry. When new buildings are built, power poles and lines must be set up to supply power for construction sites. But Moerman's pedestal can easily be installed on top of a nearby electric vault where underground power lines can be tapped for power, immediately supplying affordable power.

He recently sold more than 100 of the pedestals to a local utility company, Southern California Edison, which plans to

This affordable electric car charging station allows EV owners to power their cars at home.

lend the units to Los Angeles-area home builders. Another utility, Pacific Gas & Electric, has also bought a number of pedestals. That company rents them to general contractors building houses in its service territory.

With a little modification, the pedestal used for construction sites was turned into an affordable EV charging station. Eventually, Moerman hopes, photovoltaic panels installed at these sites will be able to power his pedestals—in this way, cars can be powered with renewable solar energy. However, even if the power used by electric vehicles is made by burning coal or oil, it is a benefit to the environment because the vehicles are not releasing pollutants caused by the burning of gasoline.

"I call it a low-tech product because it's everyday technology that meets various needs at a low cost," Moerman says. "Shopping malls could offer free charging to attract customers. And we're ready to go now. Once standards are set for the electric vehicle industry, we're ready to move."

Moerman holds two patents for his power pedestal. Each unit is constructed with a hard plastic shell and has its own electric meter. The product is manufactured at a plant in Phoenix, Arizona.

"We have to get out of this internal combustion engine mode that we're in—that's a given. We're killing ourselves, and we're killing the environment," Moerman notes. "Through legislation, we can start getting things changed, and it is happening. There is only one zero-pollution alternative known at this point that can be mass-produced—the electric vehicle. To meet these legislative mandates, we absolutely have to get this infrastructure in place—and the time is now."

For More Information

Write to Moerman Inc., P.O. Box 3053, San Luis Obispo, CA 93403, or call (805) 544-6104.

Electricity Powers "Green" Car Dealership

Green Motor Works, the nation's first electric car dealership, is up and running in Los Angeles, California, and continues to sell more and more nonpolluting electric vehicles. The dealership features a new showroom and a 1,500-square-foot production facility for converting gasoline-powered automobiles and trucks into electric vehicles.

"Everyone has some responsibility for our environmental problems," says William Meurer, owner and founder of Green Motor Works. "I believe that there is significant demand for electric vehicles among consumers and fleet operators. Every electric vehicle out there will help the environment."

Meurer worked as a photography and lighting director in Hollywood before starting Green Motor Works. After looking into the environmental problems facing the nation—and in particular in southern California—he decided to start a business that addressed the problems. He risked his own money to open the dealership in 1992.

Actor Leslie Nielsen purchased a converted Pontiac Fiero for $22,000 from the dealership. Tom Cruise has test-driven a new electric race car—with a top speed of 80 miles per hour (mph)—being sold by the firm.

Also in stock at the Green Motor Works is a converted Ford Escort with a range of 60 to 100 miles and a top speed of 65 mph. With a price tag of $18,000, the car is not cheap—but as the market for electric vehicles grows, prices will drop. "If we

Green Motor Works converted this Chevy truck from a gasoline-powered vehicle to an electric one.

had a car that cost $10,000, we could sell a ton of them," he says. "It'll take a while, but things are already moving in that direction."

Green Motor Works is currently leasing 40 Norwegian-built electric buses to the Bay Area Rapid Transit District for testing as station cars that carry passengers between various subway stations.

For More Information

Write to Green Motor Works, 5228 Vineland Avenue, North Hollywood, CA 91601, or call (818) 766-3800.

Glossary

commercialization To make available as a product or to offer for sale.

conductor A substance or device that conducts heat, sound, or electricity.

emissions Something, such as any form of gas, that is discharged. For example, gases released from the burning of coal to create electricity are forms of emissions.

extrapolation An estimation based on a known value or observation.

generator A machine that converts one form of energy into another, especially mechanical energy into electrical energy, such as occurs at most power plants.

geothermal Something that pertains to or utilizes the internal heat of the Earth.

mass transit A system of large-scale public transportation in a metropolitan area, usually composed of buses, subways, and trains.

megawatt A unit of electrical power equal to 1 million watts.

methane A colorless, odorless flammable gas obtained commercially from natural gas.

octane A designation of "anti-knock" quality in different types of gasoline; higher-octane gasoline is thought to be better for some vehicles.

opacity The degree to which a substance, such as gas, is opaque.

opaque Something that does not allow light to pass through.

ozone gas A form of oxygen produced when an electric spark is passed through air or oxygen.

perforate to make holes in

photovoltaics A form of technology involving the direct conversion of sunlight into electricity.

prefabricate To construct beforehand by manufacturing in sections, ready for quick assembly.

raptors birds of prey

renewable energy Any naturally occurring, theoretically inexhaustible, source of energy, such as solar or wind power, that does not come from fossil or nuclear fuels.

silicon A nonmetallic element having crystal-like forms that is used in the production of photovoltaic panels.

stator The portion of an electric generator that remains fixed in respect to other rotating parts.

transformer An electrical device that changes the voltage and current of electricity.

transient To last or stay only a short time.

turbine The part of an electric generator that has blades attached to a rotor that are spun by pressure, caused in many cases by steam.

Further Reading

Bailey, Donna. *Energy from Wind and Water*. Chatham, NJ: Raintree Steck-Vaughn, 1990.

Brooke, Bob. *Solar Energy*. New York: Chelsea House, 1992.

Gardner, Robert. *Experimenting with Energy Conservation*. Danbury, CT: Watts, 1992.

Goldin, Augusta. *Small Energy Sources: Choices That Work*. Orlando, FL: Harcourt Brace, 1988.

Gould, Alan. *Hot Water and Warm Homes from Sunlight*. Berkeley, CA: Lawrence Science, 1992.

Rickard, Graham. *Solar Energy*. Milwaukee, WI: Gareth Stevens, 1991.

———. *Wind Energy*. Milwaukee, WI: Gareth Stevens, 1991.

———. *Bioenergy*. Milwaukee, WI: Gareth Stevens, 1991.

Index

Photo Credits

Cover: DOE/NREL - PIX #00262, Warren Gretz; pages 8, 9: Courtesy of KTAO; page 11: Southern California Edison, an Edison International Company; pages 13, 14: PVUSA Project, Pacific Gas and Electric Company; page 18: Lila Chahroudi; pages 20, 21: Emily J. Will; page 23: The SunPipe Company; page 26: DOE/NREL - PIX #00400, Warren Gretz; page 28: DOE/NREL - PIX #00334, Warren Gretz; pages 30, 31, 35, 36: KENETECH Windpower, Inc.; pages 39, 40: Los Alamos National Laboratory; pages 41, 42: Network Energy; page 46: Solar Survival Architecture; page 47: A. Stegmeyer; pages 51, 52: Natural Gas Vehicle Coalition; page 54: SMUD; page 55: George Turner/SMUD; page 57: Moerman Inc.; page 60: Green Motor Works. Artwork by Blackbirch Graphics, Inc.